I0116767

NATYRE BOY

DEREK R. KING

Natyre Boy

Second Edition © 2025 Derek R King
First edition published in 2021 (ISBN 978-0-9992523-5-2)
Second edition ISBN 978-1-965455-06-7
eBook available

All rights reserved. No part of this publication may be reproduced, stored or transmitted in any form or by any means, electronic, mechanical, photocopying, recording, scanning, or otherwise without written permission of the publisher, except in the case of brief excerpts used in critical articles and reviews. It is illegal to copy this book, post it to a website, or distribute it by any means without permission.

Derek R. King asserts the moral right to be identified as the author of this work.

This is a work of fiction. Names, characters, places and incidents are either the products of the author's imagination or used fictionally. Any resemblance to actual persons, living or dead, events or localities is entirely coincidental.

Image Credits
Cover Art: "The Campsie Fells from Barrhill," mixed media by Jane Cornwell. www.janecornwell.co.uk

Interior photographs by Derek R. King

Interior formatting by Nicole Scarano
www.fiverr.com/nicolerscarano

CONTENTS

To and for my Muse, as always and forevermore

ACKNOWLEDGMENTS

The author warmly thanks Sarah at 8N Publications for bringing the first edition of this work into the world in 2021 (ISBN 978-0-9992523-5-2). As my second poetry collection, it remains especially dear to me—for I am, and will always be, the Natyre Boy.

My deepest gratitude to my lovely wife, author Julie Kusma, whose encouragement inspired me to reshare them as this second edition.

V

GIFTS

"I am the sun, and the moon
the air and the soil.
I am the oceans,
seas and waters.
I control the ebb and flow
of the tides of life.
I give life to trees, plants,
flowers and beasts."

As she said all this,
I hung my head
not in shame or fear
but respect.
For what is it all
without respect?
These things, these gifts
of water, of life to be,
the being
and life giver
is all.

NEW MONTH

A new month
brings new hope.
Spring bulbs push through
rich brown soil.
Weather's gloomy
grey and stormy.
Crocus, iris, snowdrops,
don't seem to care.
Their vibrant colours
blow though
the grey clouds of
my mind.

SGURR AN EILEIN GHIUBHAIS
(NR MALLAIG)

A gentle breeze
then all is still.
The little burn
gently spills.

I reach the crest
of the craggy hill,
clomp of hooves
then all is still.

I stand and stare
and so do they
the sight of deer
off to play.

LUNCH BUDDY
(LOST VALLEY, GLEN COE)

"Ooh that's a lovely sandwich.
Could you spare a beak-sized bite?
I've been up with our little ones
for most of all last night.

Gosh is that an apple?
It looks so big from here,
could you spare a tiny bit?
Aw, you're very kind my dear."

SKYE

A place of contradictions this island is
where bracken on the hillside glows
golden captured by the sun's rays, and yet
sun is obscured behind greying skies!
While azure blue seas chop to and fro
before lapping softly against the shore.
As sheets of rain drift like
delicate curtain drapes
across this landscape.

Vast hills and mountains rise
above black ribbon roads,
like sentinels guarding or
brooding parents
protective of what lies beyond.
Vetting each traveler who passes,
checking their intent.

The waterfall fulsome, fast flowing,
cascades over rocks and falls.
Even small streams and burns flow
in frenzied exuberance,

spilling occasionally beyond guiding
rocks that line their way.
Waters tumble carelessly
against grassy banks
full of vigour and purpose,
pushing towards the machair
and reed bed wash
which soothes their energies
and restores the calm.
satiated, the now gentle stream
meanders
to
the sea.

SEA LOCH AND STEADINGS
(LOCH SLIGACHAN)

High above the sea loch
a bright glowing silver moon
in darkening sky,
framed between
dark peaks to the west
towering steep over rock
and moor.

Choppy waters,
in tones of blue-grey
crowned with white
crests of frothy lace
that come and go.
Ebb and flow.

Trace the shoreline,
distant outcrops
jagged rocks
soothed by peaceful waters
bathe in a dapple light glow
from crofts and steadings

twinkling in evening's
dimming light.

FULL OF PORPOISE
(A PORTREE TREAT)

The sea grey green water
broken only occasionally
by a dorsal fin or
silky black back
when a school of porpoises
enter the bay.
They cackle into life
with cheeky chatter.
Each trying to outdo the other
They come and go in a group,
racing
the wee fishing boats to
the harbour,
which stop to greet
and throw a fish or two
caught this night to
their playful companions
with smiling gaze.

PARADISE

I come here often
to take the peace,
to sup the tranquil.
I have no special interest
just to be is suffice.

The short path
a world unto its own.
Flanked initially
by high reaching gorse and
laburnum,
settling to a pretty
avenue of colourful wild flowers.
Large and small
whites, pale blue, pinks
and purple hues
with their frequent visitors
butterfly, bees and more.
The aura and vista of this place
in cinematic like proportions
it is simply exquisite
and divine.

TITANIA

The heady scent from the brassica napus flower
fills my senses,
intoxicates my mind
easing me into gentle
heavenly
slumber and
Titania's loving bowery.

This deep seduction
gives rest to my
weary soul, and
draws me down to
sweet surrender's sleep.

A tranquility descends
soothing
and dreamy,
settles and
eases my spirit.
This blanket of tender bliss
envelopes me,

giving comfort for
I find peace within it
and I long for it.
This painfully short
spell in bloom.

CURLEW

The familiar "whooping" call of the curlew
is the first to reach my ears.
I am not sure why
but it makes me smile,
and glad that I've come here.

GRACEFUL

A gentle disturb,
puts them
to flight.
A graceful
floating magic carpet.
Colours light and
colours dark,
rise and fall with
gentle beat.
Some pass
my ear.
Elegant and serene,
they rise and halt,
a little reprieve before
they gently descend
once more.

RESPITE

I take in hand
the little yellow flower's
silky soft petal.
Gently, carefully,
not to harm
not to lift,
pick or damage,
but softly, lightly
as if a breath
of warm summer breeze
caresses it.
Finger tips,
a feather's touch,
but I still sense the feel.
Distant and longing,
a memory gifted
I treasure
in my respite.

GORSE

The almond like scent
from the gorse,
invades my psyche,
as I wander down
this bright yellow
spiky avenue.
Where sticky willows
fight for light
and soft silky wildings
petals, bonnet-like,
with lovely cheeks,
conceal the modesty
the bees seek.
The weaving heat haze
a mirage-like form,
drifts sinuously,
carrying with it
the almond like scent

GLORIANA

It is time to move?
Is there time to stay?
Linger a while
to hear once more
sweet birdsong and
rustling grasses.
To feel once more
the gentle breeze,
the sun upon my face
and breathe in the scent of
spring meadow blooms.
To tarry and
watch small insects
graceful glide
in darting flight
and while away
under clear blue sky,
until again.

FURIES OF SEA

When thundering waves
are all around
and clacking boulders the
dominant sound,
white foam filled furies
rant and rave
shattering,
splattering,
in madness depraved,
they breathe upon
wave upon
wave.

VOICES UPON THE WAVES

I hear the cry and
words of
close friends
lost to life
carried on
breaking seas.

From gentle slumber they
awaken
rekindling their vitality
through
crashing waves and yet…

They beckon to me
to make
ends meet
and share
their world.

I hear the cry and
words of

close friends
lost to life...
but not this day
sun or not...

ABSOLUTION

Cresting waves race
to greet you
do not resist,
give in to their
sweetest surrender
for they will carry
you
home.

DAWN

To greet the dawn
the blazing sun
that kissed the sky
and made it blush
that warmed the earth
its fruits to grow
that touched the hearts
love's seeds to sow.
To dance around
spring maypole dear
with hearts aflutter
a loving tear
in love's delight
the sun will pass
and greet the night
for love shall last.

BÆBES

We kissed 'till dawn
as babes in love
in spring time.

Whilst fields of
flowers came alive
glistening with
morning dew
bursting forth
with colour anew.
To caress us baebes
with petals soft
the warming dew
our sleep to bathe off.

HOPEFUL

Would you like to sail
on a sea of passion,
on a moonlit night
while the faint stars shine?

Would you like to drift
on an ocean of love and
let the soothing motion
cleanse our souls.

In loving embrace
we'll drift together
on stars and tides
forever, divine.

TRUST

I feel the stars and
the nighttime breathes.
Filling the void,
taking the seed
across the galaxy,
hand in hand.
Beyond the stars
beyond the sands
across far space
deep and wide
gone to speak
gone to hide.
Dark in caverns
yet bright with dust,
kiss the sunset
in Love we trust.

REVELRY

Dionysus,
my cup
if you please,
that I may into
this night
gently ease.
And taste the
divine
'til the
moon does
fade.

Then
come the dawn
pray
lay me to rest
in Titania's bowery
once more
to be blessed.

SUMMER'S EVE

When you hold my hand,
you hold my heart.
When you look into my eyes,
you become my part.
We walk together
shoulder to shoulder
arm in arm.
Joined together for
we are in love
this Summer's eve.

VI

SUMMER

The wax and wane of
Summer moon.
The bright and warm
summer Sun.
Glorious fauna
and spectacular flora.
The gentle sound,
of birdsong clear.
The rolling waves
upon the shore.
All of these things
and many more,
bring forth
contented sigh.

STARRY NIGHTS

Come on baby,
let's go down to the beach
let's sit on the sands
watch the tides,
gently ebb
watch the tides,
gently flow,
holding hands and
kissing as we go.
Let's swim on through
the starry night and
dance upon the sand
the moonlight at our feet,
on this long hot loving
summer night.

HEALING

When you come to this place
best bring your soul,
for the peacefulness is
something to behold.
Open up your mind and
clear your thoughts.
Take your time,
indulge this scene.
Permit the heady scents to
flood your senses and
their healing powers
cleanse your soul.

FAERIE QUEEN

In the bowery drapes the
stamen entice
waiting to caress,
to be caressed
in passion folds of
gentle petals
and longing fonds.
High in the canopy
soft hues of mellow
blossom colour
whose scent soothes me
drifts me to
another place
to be, where
faeries wings await, they
gently mop my brow
I succumb, I…
surrender
to sweet slumber's bliss
under the comfort
and soothing of
my Faerie Queen.

THE COOL SUBDUE

Warm summer breeze
drifts wearily
through the arbour.
Fonds flutter sleepily,
while Spanish moss hangs
dreamily from
the branches
of the trees.

PETALS

Flowers,
flowers,
everywhere.
The aroma of fresh
lain petals,
upon the carpet,
upon the stairs.
The scent of
fresh cut flowers
and innocence,
in her hair.
A scent of roses,
lingers there.

BOTANICAL

Genius or fool?
The thought crept into
my head
before I knew.

The explosion
of colour from
flowering borders
dazzled
in bright summer
afternoon sun.

Tall heads on elegant stalks
weaving briskly
in the freshening breeze
an infusion of
sweet perfumes
upon it.

Their bright and sensuous
seductive sway
all shapes,

all sizes,
all colours.
Flower-heads,
seed-heads,
tufties and
fauna, ripe and
green and
variegated.

Genius or fool?
The longest herbaceous border
in the world is at
Direlton Castle
Genius, methinks.
But I don't fancy the weeding!

RISE AND SHINE

The dawn chorus of gulls
greets the new,
as day breaks the night.
A harsh and noisy
cacophony, for
those deep
in slumber,
loudly
awakened.
This,
their invitation to
join the day.

POSEIDON'S LANDS

I sense the aroma of Poseidon's lands
the sharp salty tingle
arouses my mind
and demands attention.

Rounding the pathway,
I cross the flowering
machair where
periwinkle and sea pink
dance in gentle breeze.

The mocking chorus of seabirds
far ahead, greets my ears.
To some it is shrill maybe,
to me a warm welcome
from old friends.
They herald my arrival
to the sea.

The periwinkle and sea pink
dwindle now
as marram grass begins its

ascent dune ward.
Coarse but soft
it weaves a dance
until sand revealed and then
the sea.
Poseidon's land.

Sometimes blue,
sometimes grey,
but today it is green.

Sea foam horses race
each other to
reach the shore.
Leaping onto rocks to
gain advantage.
Gentle, small and sudden peaks
delicate as white lace
adorn waves crests.

While high above
sea birds glide
serenely on warming
thermal waves, above
Poseidon's lands.

SERENE, GENTLY SLEEP

Dune sea grasses
rustle softly and
sweetly sing
in my ear.
Their gentle song
caresses my
weary soul
while soft sand
folds around me
welcoming me
into its arms.
The gentle breeze
soothes
my troubled brow.
Under the sun,
calming warmth
passes into me
I drift slowly
into sleep,
deep peaceful sleep.

ODE TO JOY

I feel the sandy air
brush against my cheeks,
sea spray salt mingled in.
I hear the seaside symphony
of joyous sounds.
I see the fine sands
brushed in madness
snaking and shimmering,
its gentle sound as
it gently grounds.
I feel the wind brush
against my cheek, once more
while sun beats
upon my back.
I know this moment
will never last, but
I wish,
it will never pass.

SHANDWICK (PICTISH) STONE

Against summer's rich blue sky
the ancient Pictish stone
stands true and fast,
weather worn and beaten.
Encased in glass protection, which
only hints at the
mystery of a past where,
through glass crystal clear,
the village below appears
beneath the seas.
Waves lap over roof and
white washed walls,
clearly seen.
Hollow steel columns
stand sentinel still, holed
while encircling guide wires,
growl in the biting wind
like some ancient
ambient didgeridoo
ringing out faint majestic sounds.
Nature's harmonics through
man-made holes,

an eerie scene.
While the lapwing
chatters and converses
in the opposite
green grass field,
bringing past
and present
together.

MEADOW

The meadowland wash is so peaceful
save the birdsong in the air.
I do not know the species but
I am glad that they are there.

The grasses, reeds and hogweeds
sway gently in the breeze,
the occasional buzz of a passing insect
comes and greets my ear.

All else is quiet and peaceful.
All else is tranquil and still.
As I gaze across the machair from
my vantage point upon the hill.

PEEBLES (I)

I was just a boy when I was here.
I cried real tears on sunny days,
from bangs and scrapes and
other mischiefs of play.

In Haylodge Park
we laughed and played
in summer sun.
We ran and hid behind
ancient trees and
paddled in
the river Tweed
kicking the silty stoney bed (ouch).
Guddling for trout and
netting for minnows
with a Jack and Jill pail
in warming summer breeze.

Across three bridges
we did dare
to the other side
and the far-off lane.

Tramped home we did
with tired wee legs.
Too tired to walk
and too tired for bed.

A summer treat
as we walk home
the ice cream shop!

Their confectionary had
a distinctive taste
and glorious raspberry sauce
drizzled from a little bottle
with a long spout.
I can still taste that now,
it makes me smile,
as I sense its cold run
dribble down
my little chin.
"Hello Tiger," they said.
It bucked me up to hear that,
a stranger with nice words,
because Tigers and ice cream go
together when you are 4!

THE PEACEFUL COOL

In the broiling heat of
The Borderlands,
I seek out dapple shade of
green leaved trees.
Shelter and respite from
this taxing heat
beating down.
The warm breeze
rustles the leaves
breaking the still
but offers no relief,
save calming sounds.
The river bubbles and splutters
on its way
cool and inviting
spilling over rock
and stone.
Cool and
clear and
tempting.

ENTOMOLOGY - LESSON 1

Things with legs and
things with wings
things that buzz and
things that sting.

Things with stripes and
things with spots
some have antennae and
some have not.

DRAGONFLY - THE ART NOUVEAU

Hello little dragonfly
with your amber stripy tail.
You seem to want me to follow you
as you zig zag down the lane.

You pause and pose
then hover close.
How strange I must look
to you.

You fly ahead
but turn to check if
I'm still in
your view.

You rest upon my shoulder
peering at me
from below,
You tilt your head and
seem to say, "How strange!"
Before you go.

BUMBLEBEE

I see the tiny bumble bee
alight from here to there.
I hear its gentle humming
and softly beating wings,
as it off and humble-bumbles
through the warming summer air.

BUTTERFLY GARDEN

Butterfly Garden
lasts only an hour.
A floorshow, a carpet,
like surreal flowers
alighting en-mass from one
knapweed to another.
A flurry of colour
in rhythmic beats.
A mirage of tiny puppets
chasing from
flowerhead
to flowerhead.

OYSTERCATCHER
(NR DORNOCH)

A mid-morning treat,
I remember it well.
It was really very sunny
and hot as ....

The wee oystercatcher
was seeking shellfish to eat.
While I was wilting
in the summer heat.

With the tide coming in
it was perched on rock
watching real closely
and taking stock.

When all of a sudden
it darted with haste
spearing its bill for its
first morning taste.

SUMMER NIGHT SENSATIONS

Summer night sensations
crackles with energy,
fizzing with life.
Breathe in the hearing
air's wonderland.
Warm static every night
summer night sensations.

SUMMER SERENADE

With a pocket full of stardust
and moonbeams for our light
let's go dancing in the sand
on this long hot summer night.
Let's cross the bridge
and play our song
drifting, dancing
all night long.
Holding tight to
watch the stars
gently drift across
evening sky.
But only when the sun
breaks through
shall sleep be had
be me and you.

SHANGRI-LA

The lovers share their feelings
as the sun goes down to rest.
Sharing memories together
Of the times they remember best.

"Fading dreams
they'll last forever,
memories of you
times spent together."

They toast to endless happiness
and never ceasing love,
as they lie upon the silken grass
counting silver stars above.

VII

AUTUMN BECKONS

The day is dark when
summer falls
and cold winds blow
stripping foliage from trees.
While thickening skies
of darkest grey
grow booming, threatening
overhead.
It is time
to hibernate,
and make our winter's bed.
Away from the biting cold
and freezing rains,
which take nature to its bed.

MORNING

The clear water pools
on the harbour wall
betray the storm from
the night before.

The lone bee hums
in early morning sun
among the ferns that
grow and prosper
along cracks
and cervices of
the harbour's old
stone wall.

Soft sea waves lap gracefully
against the pontoon jetty.
Only the gentle creak and ease
of moorings
break silence still.

A single gull struts dominantly
across wet sands

puffed up and proclaiming
"These sands are mine."

Sea grasses rustle in
warm, gentle breeze.
While blue bells and
sea asters peer between,
sheltered and protected,
ofttimes from harsh sea winds.

BUTTERFLY

The butterfly
in gentle flyht
like a paper puppet on
strings so tight
fleets off to left,
and then to right
landing so softly,
with wings upright.

ENTRANCED

What draws me to you,
I know not.
Small soft fonds conceal
sharpest thorns.
Perhaps your golden yellow flower
abundance like a torch or
the sweet scent you bear
almond-esque,
a delight.
It lingers but
not too heady,
yet fills the senses
with blissful thoughts.

ITSY BITSY

Poised, pensive and waiting
swaying to and fro
on the complex silken rigging
of the sticky spider's web.
Black and beige with
outstretched legs
waiting for the call,
a tensioning web.
I only see you at first,
large, plump,
two white circles on your back
simply give you away.
My eyes adapt to your
darkened lair,
one more cousin is revealed
rigging set a respectful
distance away.
In the dark, it too clinging
to its web
waiting in hope.
And deeper and darker
and further yet,

two more relatives revealed.
Black and green stripes run
across one's back,
another completes the scene.
Very small and very bright
in its lime green coat,
on a teeny tiny little web.
It also waits
hoping to catch
any trespassers.

CLOUD WATCHING

Thick grey
foreboding
menacing
hanging
heavy laden
darker, brooding.
Sunlight
falls upon them.
Towering tall
to white puffs
and wisps
rising higher
above to a
subliminal
conscious.
The Cumulonimbus Ascent.

AUTUMN'S SIGNALS

Sun's rays beat
upon my back.
A cool breeze from
rolling hills
breathes gentle airs.
Carrying with them
faint aroma of
sweet and pleasant
woodsmoke,
from crackling fire set
to ease the chill
in stone-built steading,
at the foot of the hill.

55°47'00.9"N 3°01'52.8"W

(OR EN ROUTE FROM MIDDLETON TO
INNERLEITHEN)

On my right I have the Sun
mellow and dapple,
contemplating the set,
the end of another day.

On my left I have the Moon
bright white light, the
old man's face in silver grey,
not full but two thirds.

Both Sun and Moon
in the sky together
at the same time?
As a clock face, 10 to 2
It is a curious thing!

It is a strange season,
that brings both
so close together.
Strange but wondrous,
otherworldly,
and a beautiful sight.

AUTUMN SEAS

Across the golden harvest scene
a star on the horizon,
but trouble in the air.
Dark and thunderous
rolling in
and rolling over.
Grey green wave,
upon grey green wave
engulf the rocks below.
Tormented white tentacles
unrelenting
reaching out,
searching for more.
Filled with frothing
seething rage,
and madness
crash upon the rocks below.

They form far out at sea,
gathering pace and
fury, they roll in.
Serenely concealing their rage

foaming tideline stretches
beyond my sight
undulating,
mesmerising
crawling,
feigning,
reaching.

Sudden thunder-like rumbling, broken
only by the dull sound
like a sharply closing
blanket box
as solid wall of wave meets
solid wall of rock.

The sound
of broken wave fragments
flowing, splashing
on the rocks from on high.
Waves caramelised in colour and
seaweed strewn,
roll into shingle cove.

Slowly it withdraws
first clanking
larger stones
then, the
shshshshshs of
shingle dances.
Then and only then
the waves recede.

HARBOUR

Dark currents gather in the harbour,
deep and proficient,
barely ripple on the surface,
telltale signs of danger below.
Small circles spiral
down the depths.
Still dark, waters move
mercilessly towards
the sanctuary of the harbour.
Prowling and menacing,
within the safety of the walls,
waiting for the unsuspecting.
Ripple edge of the outer sparkle
in gentle entwine, to caress,
and soothe, in bright
sunlight, gone to
depths unseen
all gone in
an instant.

ROAR

The heavy seas,
foam and
froth and roar,
in deepest green
crashing forward
lifting sand and silt in
light brown hues.
Yachts scurry for safe harbour,
the swell rises and falls.
Crashing hard,
wave upon wave
unrelenting,
never ending,
pushing forward,
pushing forward,
no ferry today.
Tiny white monsters
surf the waves
come, crashing down
crashing down
their roar is deep,
their roar is loud.

STORMY SEAS

Who pays the ferryman?
That's what I want to know.
When summer's gone
and winter storms
rage dark and cold.
Tides are high
fierce and wild
winds howl and
shriek
like banshees.
Dark monsters
lurk
deep below
hidden
depths of
seas.

THETIS

I talk to the sea
she listens to me.
Wave upon wave
her arms
reach out toward me,
to hold me.
Her long white fingers
ripple and
undulate
beckoning me to her, to
envelope me in
her being.
To soothe and caress me.
I feel her
teasing caress
gently lapping at
my toes.
soft and serene.

I hear her call,
I see her
ever closer,

ever close.
Beckoning to me
I am ready,
to fight
no-more,
to join her.

DANCING SANDS

Starlight, cold desert sand
icy wind upon my face,
blows through my hair.

In the cool air
grains of sand dance
and weave.

In moon kissed spirals
they gently drop
into a sea of sand.

AUTUMN BERRIES

The hawthorn like bush
is bountiful
berries plump and
fiery red, hanging
brightly against
oak like leaves.
From Arabella to Hill of Fern
hawthorn after hawthorn
line this road like an avenue.
Their rich fruit glowing
Brightly in the early
autumn sun.

GIANT BELOW GROUND

It heaved and breathed
the beast below
shifting trees,
swaying to and fro.

Without a rupture
it ebbed and flowed
the moss and grass knoll,
gently rolled.

And quickly then
it ceased to last
one mighty burp,
from the troll laid in the grass.

COLQUHAR

The wind is howling
it is strong folding
grasses to the ground.
Clouds spill across the sky,
golden at the edges where
the mellow sunlight high above
kissed their skirts.
Undersides laden with
purple hue but golden edged.
Winds, strong carry them but
make no sound.
Fence line wisps of
grassy clumps
dance energetically
in these winds
their golden seed heads
animate their appearance.
Black in silhouette
against leaden sky,
two hawks glide
above the valley floor
searching for sustenance

on the heather heath
moorland below.
A second pair arrive,
trespassers!
Food is scarce in this
hardening landscape.
The first pair rise high
upon the wind
gaining advantage
banking left, a
rapid descent
sidelong
towards unwelcome guests.
Its black silhouette lost
on the heath below.
Seconds pass then
swiftly rises,
twisting turning,
fighting the wind
until talon to talon
they are locked,
deft flick,
turning spiraling down,
low
swooping,
wings, blades in the sky,
change direction.
A tilt here,
a lit there,
vying for position,
position for possession,
twisting black shapes,
turning and then
conceded.
Unwelcome guests
meekly retreat

escorted from this place,
just to be sure.
The defender returns
to his mate
to continue their search
for food
in this harsh
inhospitable place.

HARVEST SCENE

The hay bales lie motionless
in stubble fields.
Carefully placed, neat
large round bales
rest and nestle,
quiet and still.
A perimeter cordon of
Evergreen pine
and mature forest
guard their treasure
of the plains.
High in the sky
beyond the golden edge
of pale lilac ribbon cloud,
The old man in silver
harvest moon looks down
upon this age-old scene.

OF FIELDS AND MOORS

The mellow harvest sun
casts its dapple glow
across the hillsides
of cropped fields.
Golden now, they are too.
Another year, another
harvest to give thanks for.
For it is the bounty of the land.
Beyond the hedgerow
grasses turned yellow
by this season, meet
wild rugged heath.
Brown heather clumps
crawl across the hill face
providing some protection
from the elements for
small birds and mammals.

BY THE WATER'S EDGE

The peaceful serene of the water's edge
broken only by rasping pheasants
from coppice behind,
gives form to the voices of nature.

Small white clouds, grey clouds,
speckle blue autumn sky.
A solitary, spindly,
wispy cloud
drifts by.
Thin, like a black smoke trail.

I hear the familiar call of geese,
but they're nowhere to be seen.
Lying low and sheltered, most likely
in some grassy bank
above the water's edge.
I watch and listen and
drink in this scene.

FLOWING RIVERS

I miss the flowing river,
babbling brooks and
gurgling streams.
But if I close my eyes
real tightly
and open my ears
I'm at that scene.
For nothing's lost
that's not forgotten,
just open our minds
so we might see,
the precious things
we thought were lost
like flowing rivers
babbling brooks
and gurgling streams.

LOST FOR WORDS

In the distance
snow-capped mountains
mellow late autumn morning sun
caressing their summits.
Sunlit ribbons of grey
blue puffy cloud drift
lazily behind.

Wearily each mountain's details
slowly revealed in
shades of light and dark grey.
Gullies, fissures, corries
craggy features,
worn with age of
countless millennia.

Trees of every shape and colour
to my left and right.
Leaves firmly holding on,
stand testament
to the hardiness,
of the summer canopy.

Foliage in shades of dapple
yellows and golden hues,
and more,
fiery reds and ochres
adorn tall slender trees.
hang crisply in determined grip
for as long as they can.

Branches, curving
reaching stretching,
almond shaped,
themselves seemingly flickering
lapping upwards
in the gentle wind,
rustling and rattling
like flames in
a crackling fire.
Some ripe with plump red berries
a signal to wildlife,
'store of energy,'
survival for some.

Among this racket and clamour
quiet and subdued but no less graceful
the evergreens, quiet and content.
Changing seasons mean little
to their canopy.
Their blossoming fruit develops
into cones, some plump,
some slender, elongated cones.
A marvel of nature's engineering.
Armour plated, each protecting,
concealing a wafer-thin nature's seed.
Serene, gently swaying,
billowing gracefully,
slow motion like

in the season's winds.
Each tree tall proud and erect,
standing to attention,
watching over these
seasonal changes.

VIII

GEESE

I saw the geese in flight
this still December morning,
across faint pink and blue sky,
I'm sure it means something.

It's late in year and bitterly cold
but they don't seem to mind.
Elegant necks,
long and
outstretched,
roll forward with
every beat of
their wings.

Slow regular
serene and majestic
they move.
They are twelve
a flying "V"
graceful
ever onwards
gently beating.

WINTER MORNING

The peace of it will
have you weary.
The tranquillity will
make you leery.
For time is short
but pressure great
no time to fear
this Heaven's gate.

To face the call
of dawn's new waking
to seize the day,
not slip away.
Days are precious and
not to be lost,
no mistaking.
And when time and tide in
nighttime clash,
replaying angry and
resentful scenes
to the last,

be humble and calm
and serenely wait
no time to fear
Heaven's gate.

CONTEMPLATION

How many before me
have stood here
looking out across this sea?
How many before me
in decades and centuries past
have done the same as me?
And how many more will follow us
and stand right here and gaze?
For time and tide and sunlight
hold fast for no ordinary mortal man.

WINTER'S EVE

The unmistakable crunch
of frosted earth
is music to my ears.
It is both reassuring and welcome,
for there are no other sounds here.

Some birds of the air sit
in tree tops high, basking
sunlit and warm.
The odd rustle of leafy bush
by tiny bird, clear, but
I can't be sure.
Small mouse, stoat or
weasel? Perhaps.
But no ground creature is about,
it's bitterly cold
for their tiny feet
to thread their way
through undergrowth,
this icy day.

MID-WINTER SUNLIGHT

There is a low sun today,
barely reaches above the horizon
not even level with
low barren tree tops
in the distance.

It casts its pale mid-winter light
across fallow grass plains,
where pale dry grasses
mingle with a solitary fir.

As the sun begins its
gentle release of
the frost bound,
gentle scent
of the grasslands
begins to rise,
faint, but
very recognisable
for all that, and
blissful,
despite the cold.

WALKING ON WATER

Red rowan berry
on darkened brown branch
holds its fruit until the last.
The birds of flight are grateful
for there are slim pickings here.

Swans, geese, ducks, gulls and crow,
all walk upon the water this day,
their pond succumbed to
Jack Frost's Magic wand.

Frozen it is,
but for a corner spared.
Somewhere to drink from
for the fowl of the air.

The buzzard however,
sits in the high tree,
bathed in sunlight,
overseeing the scene.

But the narrow wee burn

fast flowing on its way
escapes Jack's frost,
too fast for Jack,
on this particular day.

So much to see,
so much to tell.
I implore you to alight
from your soft and warm
comfy cell.
Come share the joy
of this nature's scene
for Jack's frosty wand,
paints a picture serene.
And just to be sure,
in case he's about
some warm mulled wine
will keep him out.

FOREST FLOOR

Patches of unmelted snow
lie on the forest floor
like discarded linen.
Pristine white, and crisp still
crackling underfoot.
A lingering sign
of the winter weather
which passed this way.
Harvested trees,
discarded bark,
twigs of all sizes
a fine latticework,
glisten icy with snow.
Stumps remain, firmly
holding to the earth
sprinkled with the fallen
needles from upper limbs.

Green grass as always
finds root and grows
in this now wide-open area
overhung by treetop canopy.

While pools of dank,
dark water collect in patches,
an icy layer on top.
A lone bird cries out,
it sounds forlorn.
Perhaps this clearing
was once home.

The stream gurgles and spills
across the rocks.
Peat coloured it flows
softly cascading
bubbling and gurgling
on its way, yet
rippling wildly to eventual calm,
beyond the narrow bridge.

WINTER SUN

Above the flat grassy moorland,
icy mist begins to form
between bitter cold light air
and the warmth of the Mother Earth.
Gentle at first
rising up from the grass.
Creating a soft
silvery grassy carpet,
slowly growing, creeping,
through fence and
over dyke, it claims
field after field.
Tall trees rise high above,
barren black in silhouette
against low orange ball and
fading winter sun sky,
releasing its final hold,
giving way to the moon.
Mist rising, from the flat lands
stubble and scrub growth
now fields but gone.

GLISTEN

There is no reason,
rhyme or trust
in darkened sky through
pale moonlight dust,
that clouds blow by
in hues of grey and
silver white light.

On fields below
rise up sparkling speckles
water's crystal diamonds.
They glisten below
from icy caress, a
cold dark hand,
envelops the green
across the lands and
begs the question
it's dark tonight
who's not alone?

SNOWY MORNING SUNRISE

We've had snow
We've had snow
Two foot deep
So nowhere to go.

We've had snow
But I'm not complaining
At least it's sunny
And it's not flippin' raining.

CHRISTMAS LIGHT

The Christmas light
is bright inside me,
I have no tree or,
tinsel to see.

Wonderful friends
I have around me,
my passion is deep,
for humanity.

ELF-ING HANDS

I'm an elf
I'm an elf
On Santa's shelf.

Wrappin' and packin'
with ribbons & bows
working so hard
only 5 days to go.

CHRISTMAS MORNING

Santa's coming,
reindeer calling.
On the sleepy world
Snow is falling.

Spreading joy,
happiness abounds,
with each flake of snow
that graces the ground.

All wrapped up warm
and sound asleep.
The children wait
as the snow grows deep.

Dawn is calling,
the children rise.
Deep snow is glistening
like the joy in their eyes.

MAGPIE V CAT

The black and white magpie
taunts the black and white cat,
mocking the feline, while
perched high in the tree on the
slender most branch.
It goads the cat,
fixated in trance
(and not at all happy I might add!)

Bright petrol blue green feathers
attract the sun and glisten,
bright like a flash.
The cat however has less to say.
Much more precarious
on a branch that strains heavily
under the weight of the cat's
Christmas Day.

But no less arrogant
of its superiority,
for all that.
The cat sits transfixed

staring
at its would-be prey.

It paws for a higher branch
the lower one springs
cat settles back down
and begins to think.

Until at last,
the magpie calls
"Not today"
beats its wings,
alights the scene.

The cat remains, pensive
poised and perched,
no longer the magpie
to fill its thoughts,
suddenly aware
of its perilous plight
as the branch it rests on,
slips further down,
under its weight.
At once the cat,
sets eyes on the stream
flowing below it.
A high pitch 'meow' it
now emits,
precariously perched
above the
stream
now realising the
folly of
this hunt.

NEW YEAR'S DAY

Jack Frost has been busy last evening
painting bushes and shrubs.
Small waxy berberis leaves, covered
with delicate crisp white spines of frost,
edges trimmed, picked out in low
bright early morning January sunlight
glow and shine, radiantly, efflorescently.
Each leaf illuminated by sun's touches
in a bright white crisp glow.
A beautiful sight this dawn, it
glistens, sparkles and twinkles and
dazzles to greet the eyes
in glorious splendour
of sun on high.
For cold it surely is
but there is beauty to behold
it is so much more than
simply,
"Brrr, it's cold!"

PEEBLES (II)

I was just a boy when I was here.
In winters cold,
fingertips were numb.
tingling with icy cold
Collecting cones and
sycamore seeds
to see those fly
when tossed in air
how wonderful to
my child's eye.

BE-CALMED

Some minutes of peace
I manage to steal,
caught between my own
heart's desires
and the seemingly relentless
cycle of work.

A few minutes of peace
appear,
like a soft and
gentle lullaby amidst
a storm of chaos.
Sitting quietly
beside the Loch-side
I steal a while.

FROST

Fragile rime patterns
upon my window pane.
Trace the path of
memories
and long sought
dreams.
Geometric structures
dance and glisten
in sunlight.
Their frost tipped fingers
reach out, pointing
to follies
of the past.

13 SNOWDROPS

Snowdrops lift
their weary heads
above the frost
glazed grass.

They open up
their satin leaves
searching for
warming sunlight.

Sunbeams dance
between the trees
their branches heavy
with budding leaves.

The mist it clears
before the dawn
to welcome in
another morn.

REFLECTION

Besides family and friends,
what will you miss most,
when the end time comes?
People or possessions
your life's love, passion shared
the gentle touch,
the heavenly scent
the kindly eyes,
the knowing smile?
Some car,
some computer or
other machine?
Hyperbole superlative
performance
that thrills to the last,
until the next?
But all given life by man
or something else?

Could it be, the first bud of
snowdrop and crocus
Or daffodil and tulip

signaling signs of spring
their first bloom bursting
into colour splendour?

Perhaps the gentle lap of sea on rock?
The crackle of shingle beach?
To reach a mountain summit and
see as far as the eye can see?

To hear the beat of wings
of birds in flight,
the unmistakable call from
the eagle high above?

Maybe the fantastical colours
and sight of the butterfly,
dragonfly and more
on a hot and sunny day
as they zig zag dance
on their merry way?

Possibly the aroma of the salt sea air
in the early morn dew?
The sweet scent of new mown grass
rising in summer's dusky hours.

Or autumn time's ripe golden
fields for harvest,
the rising moon with
setting sun in sky together?
The turning of green leaves to
vivid ochres, fiery reds and
warm soothing golden hues?

Later perhaps,
icy patterns on glass or the crunch

of frozen ground under foot?
The frosted coating on leaves
Glistening in the winter sun
or crisp, in cold winter nights,
basking in moonlit glow?
Braving the hard winter's elements
to return home
to a warm welcome
and sustenance.
What will you miss the most
when the end time comes?

DUST TO DUST

To be part of nature
is all that I want.
To share the bounty
the harvest,
the barren and
the want.
It is natural this calling
whether land or sea or air
For someday it is inevitable
I shall return to thee.

LIST OF POEMS WITH FIRST LINES

V

- Respite - I take in hand the little yellow flower's silky soft petal (17)
- Gorse - The almond like scent from the gorse (18)
- Gloriana - It is time to move? It there time to stay? (19)
- Furies of Sea - When thundering waves are all around (20)
- Voices upon the waves - I hear the cry and words of close friends (21)
- Absolution - Cresting waves race to greet you (23)
- Dawn - To greet the dawn the blazing sun (24)
- Bæbes - We kissed 'till dawn as babes in love (25)
- Hopeful - Would you like to sail on a sea of passion (26)
- Trust - I feel the stars and the nighttime breathes (27)
- Revelry - Dionysus, my cup if you please that I may into this night gently ease. (28)
- Summer's Eve - When you hold my hand (29)

VI

- Summer - The wax and wane of Summer moon (33)
- Starry nights - Come on baby, let's go down to the beach (34)
- Healing - When you come to this place best bring your soul (35)
- Faerie Queen - In the bowery drapes the stamen entice (36)
- The Cool Subdue - Warm summer breeze drifts wearily (37)
- Petals - Flowers, flowers, everywhere (38)
- Botanical - Genius or fool? The thought crept into my head before I knew (39)

- Rise and Shine - The dawn chorus of gulls greets the new (41)
- Poseidon's Lands - I sense the aroma of Poseidon's lands the sharp salty tingle (42)
- Serene, Gently Sleep - Dune sea grasses rustle softly and sweetly sing (44)
- Ode to Joy - I feel the sandy air brush against my cheeks (45)
- Shandwick (Pictish) Stone - Against summer's rich blue sky the ancient Pictish stone (46)
- Meadow - The meadowland wash is so peaceful (48)
- Peebles (I) - I was just a boy when I was here (49)
- The Peaceful Cool - In the broiling heat of The Borderlands (51)
- Entomology - Lesson 1 - Things with legs and things with wings (52)
- Dragonfly - The Art Nouveau - Hello little dragonfly with your amber stripy tail (53)
- Bumblebee - I see the tiny bumble bee alight from here to there (54)
- Butterfly Garden - Butterfly Garden lasts only an hour (55)
- Oystercatcher (nr Dornoch) - A mid-morning treat, I remember it well (56)
- Summer Night Sensations - Summer night sensations crackles with energy (57)
- Summer Serenade - With a pocket full of stardust (58)
- Shangri-la - The lovers share their feelings (59)

VII

VIII

- Frost - Fragile rime patterns upon my window pane (116)
- 13 Snowdrops - Snowdrops lift their weary heads (117)
- Reflection - What will you miss most when the end time comes? (118)
- Dust to Dust - To be part of nature is all that I want (121)

ABOUT THE AUTHOR

Derek R. King is a multi-genre, award-winning poet and author, as well as a photographer and a musician. He lives in Scotland with his wife, Julie L. Kusma, where they enjoy the great outdoors, long walks in the hills, going to seaside, art, and taking pictures for some of their books.

Poetry Collections
Soulmates Forevermore (Love Poetry)
New Year's Frost (Seasonal Poetry)
Forevermore (Love Poetry)
In Sun & Shade (Nature Poetry
More Red Roses (Love Poetry)
Urban (City-Nature Poetry)
The Elegy (Dark Poetry)
Twelve Red Roses in Verse (Love Poetry)
Natyre Boy (Nature Poetry)
Noir [Or, When the Night Comes] (Gothic Poetry)

Nonfiction
The Life and Times of Clyde Kennard
(Biographical-American Civil Rights)

Follow this Author
http://DerekRKing.uk
https://x.com/DerekRKing2
https://www.instagram.com/derekrking2/

DEREK R KING
POET | AUTHOR

If you enjoyed this book, you might like…

Collaborations

Children's Concept Books
Monty's Silly Seascape
Monster Me ABCs
Vegetabites
Fruitabet
Thump! Thump!I
I Love My Alphabet
ABCs of Goblin Curiosities Alphagems:
My First 26 Gemstones Zenardi's
Carnival of ABCs
Sea of ABCs
What Might You Get? 26 Gifts of the
Alphabet Alphabites: the Alphabet One
Bite at a Time

Children's Storybooks & Picture Books
The Enchanted Summer Faerie Realm The
Literary Hedgehog
The Enchanted Faerie Realm Too
The Disgustingly foul World of Goblins
The Bee Book
Space Whales
The Enchanted Winter Faerie Realm The
Poetry Mouse
Jaggy Little Babies
The Enchanted Faerie Realm

Middle Grade
The Toaster of Knowledge

Educational Books
Our Dinosaurs: Discoveries, Distinctions, & More
(K)no(w)where: Manifestation Made Easy Our
Planets: Moons, Myths, & More
Our Trees: Botanics, Beliefs, & More

If you enjoyed this nature ramble, pray take a moment before off you amble. For if these words brought some delight, please leave a review, before you take flight.

www.ingramcontent.com/pod-product-compliance
Lightning Source LLC
Chambersburg PA
CBHW060502280326
41933CB00014B/2826

9 781965 455067